ARGENTINA

Travel Journal

UNPLUG & WRITE

WANDERLUST JOURNALS COLLECTION

WWW.WANDERLUST-JOURNALS.COM

WHEN WE TRAVEL
WE STOP BEING WHO WE ARE
TO BECOME BEING
WHO WE WANT TO BE.

AUG 7 PM

BY AIR MAIL

INDEX

If found	8
Trip Planner	11
Checklist	14
Telephone numbers	16
Packing list	18
Itinerary Overview	28
Maps	33
My favourite landscapes	36
My favourite museums	38
Restaurants I love	40
My chillout places	42
Serendipitous travel moments:	44
Things I do while traveling but not at home:	46
Songs that inspire me on this trip:	48
Cultural shock	50
Mood Tracker	52
Color me when stressed	56
My takeaway of this trip is:	61
Countries I have visited in my life...	68
My best photos	69
Wonderful people I met on this trip	80
My creative space	115

If found
please return it to:

Name:

Address:

Phone number:

Email address:

Trip Planner

W?

What? (Do I want to learn from this trip)

When? (Do I travel?)

Where? (Do I go?)

Why? (Do I travel?)

Checklist
Things to do before leaving

Family and Friends

Telephone numbers

(in case I lose my phone)

Packing list

Things I'm taking with me

Carry-on
Important Documents and Necessities

Hygiene and medicine

Clothing

Miscellaneous

Itinerary Overview

Maps

(Paste map)

My favourite landscapes

My favourite museums

Restaurants I love

My chillout places

Serendipitous travel moments:

Serendipity is an unexpected discovery when we are seeking something different.
The word emerged in 1700 from a Persian fairy tale, which takes place on an island called "Serendip", in which the protagonists solved all their problems through coincidences.

What is my Serendipitous moment in this trip?

Things I do while traveling but not at home:

Songs that inspire me on this trip:

Cultural shock
(Things, People, habits I'm not used to see)

Mood Tracker

Things that make me happy:

Things that make me sad:

Things that make me angry:

Things that make me Calm:

Color me when stressed
(or waiting at the airport)

DRAW WHATEVER IS MISSING

DRAW WHATEVER IS MISSING

My takeaway of this trip is:

I HAVE LEARNED...

For next trip I would avoid...

What I liked the most...

Countries I have visited in my life...

(TO FILL IN)

My best photos

When?

Where?

When?

Where?

When?

Where?

When?

Where?

Wonderful people I met on this trip

Name:
Email:
Country:
He / She Made my trip special because...

Name:
Email:
Country:
He / She Made my trip special because...

NAME:
EMAIL:
COUNTRY:
HE / SHE MADE MY TRIP SPECIAL BECAUSE...

NAME:
EMAIL:
COUNTRY:
HE / SHE MADE MY TRIP SPECIAL BECAUSE...

My thoughts

My creative space

Thanks for leaving a review for this book or sending us your feedback to:

contact@wanderlust-journals.com

Don´t forget to Check out

The Wanderlust Journals collection

We have a journal for every moment of your life

WWW.WANDERLUST-JOURNALS.COM

Get 30% off

On your next Wanderlust Journal
CODE: 4CTLX2K3

INSTRUCTIONS:

- Scan the QR CODE (or just enter Createspace store and search Wanderlust journals)
- In the checkout insert the code: 4CTLX2K3 and automatically save 30% in your purchase.

Copyright © 2015 Lana Barce
DESIGNED IN BARCELONA
All rights reserved.
This book or any portion thereof
may not be reproduced or used in any manner whatsoever
without the express written permission of the publisher
except for the use of brief quotations in a book review.

Made in the USA
Las Vegas, NV
11 December 2023